I Love You,
Not

JG YANS

BALBOA.
PRESS

A DIVISION OF HAY HOUSE

Balboa Press books may be ordered through booksellers or by contacting:

Balboa Press
A Division of Hay House
1663 Liberty Drive
Bloomington, IN 47403
www.balboapress.com
1 (877) 407-4847

Because of the dynamic nature of the Internet, any web addresses or links contained in this book may have changed since publication and may no longer be valid. The views expressed in this work are solely those of the author and do not necessarily reflect the views of the publisher, and the publisher hereby disclaims any responsibility for them.

The author of this book does not dispense medical advice or prescribe the use of any technique as a form of treatment for physical, emotional, or medical problems without the advice of a physician, either directly or indirectly. The intent of the author is only to offer information of a general nature to help you in your quest for emotional and spiritual well-being. In the event you use any of the information in this book for yourself, which is your constitutional right, the author and the publisher assume no responsibility for your actions.

Any people depicted in stock imagery provided by Thinkstock are models, and such images are being used for illustrative purposes only.
Certain stock imagery © Thinkstock.

Print information available on the last page.

ISBN: 978-1-5043-6989-3 (sc)
ISBN: 978-1-5043-7006-6 (e)

Library of Congress Control Number: 2016919047

Balboa Press rev. date: 12/16/2016

Acknowledgement

I would like to thank Emily Bannon, my writing coach. It was a pleasure working with you. I also would like to thank Anita A., and John G., for their belief in my work.

Even though I walk through the valley of the shadow
of death, I fear no evil, for Thou art with me.
Psalms 23:4

Dedication Page

I dedicate this book to my loving family.
Dad you are no longer with us but you will always
be my inspiration. I will always love you.
Mom, you are my strength and my rock. I love you forever.
Last but not least, Henry my brother, my better half,
you are my star, my joy, my life. I love you.

I n 1978, two weeks before Halloween, I turned to look out of the back window of the car as the tires crunched over the gravel drive. Raindrops sprinkled the window but I could still see Rosemont Academy recede into the night behind the car. After years, the nightmare of that place was finally over. Often touted as one of the most highly esteemed boarding schools since its founding in 1878, its outward reputation did not match the experience of its students.

It must have once been nice, the founders might have had high ideals for founding Rosemont in the first place, but now it felt like a little more than a fancy, private prison. I know most students feel that way about their schools, at least to some extent, but to the students of Rosemont Academy, prison might have been preferable.

Our meals were thinly rationed and there wasn't a night at school when I didn't lie awake in my dormitory, my stomach aching in the dark. Medical care was all but nonexistent and the buildings were under a tight lock and key. The instructors didn't seem to care if we studied and the gray skies of England kept everything in a dark, gloomy atmosphere that would have been better suited to a Victorian novel in which a heroine is running across the moors to find her lost love. But at Rosemont life was not a Victorian novel and there was no love to be found.

It was at Rosemont that I found my closest friends, my missing pieces. Annie was my parallel. We were both athletic, participating in the school's one team sport, soccer, which existed mostly as a public relations stunt for parents of prospective students. But the athletes received an extra meal because, of course, it wouldn't do to have athletes collapse on the field in public and tarnish the school's reputation. So, I signed up for the extra food and I met Annie, who had signed up for the love competition, food too, but mostly her competitive nature.

Annie quickly rose to team captain and I was always right behind her. She was quicksilver on the field, her long curly ponytail swishing and snapping behind her like a whip as she darted around the opposing players towards the goal. My hair, by contrast, was dark and short and my shoulders were broad, my hips narrow. I most admired Annie's tenacity; once she said she was going to do something, she followed through. She proved this follow through on numerous occasions, especially when we started trying everything we could to get expelled from Rosemont Academy. Thankfully, our parents removed us from the school before she had the opportunity to follow through on her idea to get pregnant, the one action that we believed would lead to an immediate expulsion.

Although she was ferocious on the soccer field, her heart was soft and I often found her reading romance novels.

"Once I'm out of this place," she'd say, "I'm going to marry my own Prince Charming."

"What about soccer?" I asked once when we were hanging out in our room.

"The two aren't mutually exclusive," she'd scolded me with

a smile. "I can have my picture on a Wheaties box *and* produce the most beautiful, athletic children you've ever seen."

I'd made a joke about her not having time, with the duties that come with ruling over a kingdom alongside Prince Charming, and she'd thrown her book at me. I remember picking it up and looking at the cover. It featured a handsome man on a pirate ship, his shirt unbuttoned as he clung to a rope in a storm while a beautiful damsel clung to his waist. I had no idea where she'd gotten it, this sort of literature was banned at Rosemont Academy, and yet she always seemed to have a never ending supply. This one was called *Captain of Her Storm.*

"Are you going to marry a pirate?" I asked. "Because there are no soccer fields on the ocean." She threw a pillow at me. I laughed.

Judy was blonde and beautiful. She looked most like someone who would appear on the cover of one of Annie's romance novels. She was coy and flirtatious. Annie once told her she thought Judy would make a beautiful model but Judy just shook her head. Her aspirations weren't in the glamorous world of diamonds and Dior, but instead were simple. Judy dreamed of a husband and a family, much like the home in which she'd grown up as a child. She loved the fantasy of a white picket fence around a clipped green yard in which her children played. But even now, as I look back at old photographs from those days, I'm continually awed by her beauty and although she never wanted, a part of me still wishes she'd pursued modeling. However, she never loved the camera the way it loved her.

The final member of our group was Francesca, fiery, fierce, ambitious, gorgeous Francesca. There was something about her that lit up a room, something that I grew to rely on as our time at Rosemont Academy slowly ground me down. She was so bright and effervescent and her emotions were always so honest, never tempered, for better or worse. Francesca never cared much for sports but she and Judy always watched the soccer matches, and Francesca's voice could often be heard cheering above the crowd's collective noise. Back in school, she had big dreams of becoming an actress and, we all thought, her long, dark, curling hair, beautiful face, and fit body would be just right for the silver screen. She read often but created her own stories even more frequently, acting out in animated detail in the common room of our dormitory on Sundays after the church services were done. The staff members in our dormitory were supposed to discourage that sort of thing--and they usually did--but they made an exception for Francesca, doing their best to suppress their smiles as they watched from the doorway. Francesca always seemed elevated somehow to us, like some sort of mythical goddess, and we just knew that out of all of us, she was the one destined to be someone special.

In the car on that last night when I left Rosemont Academy, I rode alone. Annie, Judy, and Francesca had already been sent for by their parents and now, it was just me. Before we'd separated, we'd exchanged addresses and phone numbers and promises to stay in touch. At the moment, I'm sure we meant it. But even so, as I watched the school fade behind the car, I had a sense that our promises were as flimsy as the sheets of notebook paper on which we'd written our contact information.

When I arrived in California, the day was bright and I felt optimistic about the possibilities I faced now that I had escaped from that horrid school. My joy, however, was short-lived when I returned home to my domineering mother whose demeanor bore a strong resemblance to the school I'd just escaped. My older brother and sister were of no help to me and my only refuge was in work. I soon found employment as a receptionist for a local law firm and my days became an endless repetition of work followed by a quiet home life that had become gray and still as I did my best to avoid my mother. At night, I would lie in my bed and look out the window at the oak tree that stood, strong and steadfast beside it. I would count the leaves instead of counting sheep as I drifted off to sleep at night, dreaming of when I'd find a love of my own to escape the dark home I'd come to know. I knew that then, finally then, I would be able to find the happier world I'd dreamed of with my friends at school. On many of those nights, as I watched the oak tree branches move in their own slow dance in the wind, I wondered about my friends. We'd sworn to keep in touch, but we hadn't. We did at first, but as we began to be consumed by our own lives, the letters had slowed until they stopped altogether. I wondered if they were conquering the big dreams they'd shared with me, if Annie was on her way to being a great athlete or if Francesca was walking the red carpet in glamorous dresses for her movie premieres. Did Judy find her white picket fence bliss? Did Annie find a beautiful pirate like the one on the covers of her romance novels? Or were they like me, sad and lonely and waiting for their real lives to begin?

About a year after I left Rosemont Academy, I attended church with my mother and siblings as we did every Sunday. The morning was gray and the sky hung with pregnant clouds although it hadn't rained, not yet. After the service ended, I stood outside the church with my family as my mother talked with her friends. Bored, I glanced around the crowd of parishioners, and then I saw him. On a day when everyone kept glancing suspiciously at the sky, he stood tall and his blond hair looked like a patch of sunlight. He seemed to sense my eyes on him and he looked over at me and smiled. I felt that smile all the way down to my toes. I watched as he excused himself from the conversation he was having and walked in my direction.

"Hi," he said, holding out his hand. "I'm David."

"Diane," I said, taking his hand to shake it. His grip was warm, confident. I glanced out of the corner of my eye at my mother but she was so absorbed in her own conversation that she didn't notice David's arrival.

"Nice to meet you," he said. He paused, looking down at his feet for a moment. Was he nervous? I couldn't tell, nor could I imagine anyone as beautiful as him ever being nervous.

"Do you . . . I know this is strange because we literally just met, but do you want to go get something to eat?" he asked.

"Now?" I asked, caught off guard.

"Yup. We'll be like everyone else after church and go for pancakes," he said. I hesitated for a moment, glancing at my mother.

"Mom, I'm going out for a while, I won't need a ride home," I said quickly to her. She looked at me and glanced over at David, noticing the intruder for the first time.

"That's fine," she said lightly, although I could tell by her expression that it wasn't but she wasn't willing to make a scene in front of her friends.

David and I left together to a nearby diner. As predicted, it was full of the after church crowd but we managed to get a small booth towards the back of the diner. We sat and talked together as the rain finally began to fall outside, tapping on the window beside our table. Our conversation lasted through pancakes and several cups of coffee and I felt like I never wanted it to end. Although we had just met that day, I felt like I'd known David for my whole life. We exchanged pieces of our lives over those pancakes. I told him about Rosemont Academy and the friends I missed so much. I learned that he was in his final year of law school, he hated peas, and that he was undoubtedly the man I wanted to marry. As he poured me what I think was my sixth or seventh cup of coffee, I logically knew that that was crazy since I'd only known him for a few hours, but every other fiber of my body felt more sure of this than I'd ever felt about anything else. When you know, you know.

Two months later, I discovered that David felt the same way I did. He took me back to that same diner and we sat in our same booth. I'd noticed he seemed distracted and I asked him if he was concerned about his upcoming bar exam.

"No. I mean, yes, I'm nervous about the bar exam, but that's not what's on my mind today," he said, glancing down at his hands, which I noticed were shaking slightly. He took a deep breath and I waited, almost afraid of what could be coming next. David reached across the table and took my hands in his.

"Diane, I love you. I've never loved anyone the way I love you. I know this is fast and I don't know what I have to offer you other than my love, but . . ." he paused, releasing one of my hands to pull a small box out of his pocket. "I already know that I don't want to live my life without you." He opened the box, revealing a small, square cut diamond set on a delicate band. Tears stood in the corners of my eyes as he slid out of his side of the booth and knelt on the floor beside mine.

"Diane, will you marry me?"

The frenzy of the diner had screeched to a halt at the sight of David on one knee, holding a ring box before me. The tension in the diner was thick as the patrons all waited for my response, their collective breath held along with his. The tears came rushing down my cheeks and I couldn't find the words so I just nodded, my face breaking into a huge grin. David kissed me then and the crowd in the diner applauded, but all I could hear was David whispering his love for me, over and over in my ear. The diner had no champagne but our server brought us milkshakes piled high with whipped cream and cherries to celebrate, starting a tradition we continued each year on our anniversary.

A year after we married, our son, Johnny, was born, followed by his sister, Heather, only two years behind him. Our lives were cozy and happy at home and my days were filled with little hands, peanut butter and jelly sandwiches, cooking, and cleaning and I'd never been happier. My only real moments of sadness came when I would, on occasion, pull out the old photos of my friends. I still felt a dull ache in my heart for Annie, Judy, and Francesca and I hoped they were happy. I had no idea how to even begin looking for them but I wished I could share all the love in my life with them.

As the kids got older, I became involved in their schools and David and I both helped with their homework. Johnny reminded me a lot of myself as he fell in love with sports, although his passion lay in baseball, not soccer as mine had. Heather was quiet and introspective and devoured books like they were air for her. Friends had warned me about the dreaded teen years but none of those predictions came to fruition. With my children becoming more and more self-sufficient, I returned to school to get my degree in psychology. With the support and encouragement of my family, I completed my degree within only two years with plans to return to school to complete my Masters. I wasn't sure how I'd ended up lucky enough to have Johnny and Heather and, most of all, David, but I prayed my luck would never run out.

The week after Heather's high school graduation, David was diagnosed with stage four prostate cancer. I did my best to hold myself together and I went into crisis management mode, scheduling chemotherapy and radiation and taking studious notes at every meeting with David's doctors. David deteriorated quickly, losing weight until he was just a shadow of his former self. He quit his job and I took a part-time job to help bring in some extra money although it pained me to be away from David for even an hour. Heather offered to delay college for a year to stay home and help but David adamantly refused. Ultimately, it turned out not to matter.

On the reduced income, we were forced to sell our house and move into a two bedroom apartment. Lying down became increasingly uncomfortable for David so he began sleeping in his recliner in the living room. With Johnny home for the summer, I gave him our bedroom and took to sleeping on the couch, David's labored breathing a slow metronome lulling me to sleep each night. On the nights when sleep eluded me, I'd go down to our car in the parking lot, climb inside, and cry. I cried loudly, my wails filled the inside of the dark car and I sobbed until my gut ached. Finally, once my body and heart were spent, my stability would return. I would think of the oak tree that had been outside my bedroom at my childhood home, think of its strength, and I would eventually get out of the car and go back inside. A few times at nights, I awoke to hear David quietly crying in his recliner. I feigned sleep, not wanting to break this personal moment that he had clearly saved for the darkness, when no one could see him. I don't know if David ever knew about my nighttime excursions but if he did, he never said anything just as I never mentioned hearing him cry at nights. We both pretended to be a lot stronger than we actually were.

On a warm day in early August, I'd driven David to the hospital for his chemotherapy. It was our anniversary and I wanted to surprise him with a milkshake after his treatment. He had so little appetite then but I wanted to do something to show him that we were still us, that cancer could change our lives but it could never change how much I loved him. I went to a local fast food spot and ordered a couple of milkshakes, strawberry for me, chocolate for him. I smiled, remembering how many cherries the waitress had piled on top of our shakes the day David had proposed. We'd discovered later that David had accidentally knelt in spilled maple syrup when he asked me to marry him. As I drove back to the hospital, I reflected on that day, of how young and innocent we'd been. We had no idea what was in front of us, nothing about Johnny or Heather or the life we'd build together. We knew nothing except how much we loved each other.

When I returned to the hospital, carrying the milkshakes, David wasn't where I'd left him. A nurse saw my confusion and came over to get me. She led me into one of the doctor's offices where I waited until David's doctor entered. He explained that shortly after I left, David had suffered a massive heart attack but due to the DNR he had signed, without my knowledge, they had been unable to do anything to restart his heart. I don't remember dropping the milkshakes but I must have because I saw the brown and pink shakes oozing in a puddle around my feet, curling into one another when they met in the middle. I do remember apologizing profusely to the doctor for the mess who kept trying to deflect my apologies. I must have tried to clean up the mess myself because later, when I changed into my pajamas, I saw that there were milkshake stains on the knees of my jeans. It was then that I finally screamed, clutching the dirty clothes to my chest.

The funeral passed in a haze, I hardly even knew what happened. Johnny had quietly taken over the arrangements for me and I felt like I was moving underwater. I managed to pull myself together long enough to go to work but even then, I felt like I was just going through the motions. The days were okay, because at least I had my job to distract me, but the nights were long and painful and lonely. The bed felt empty, too large for me, and I found myself crying for David most nights. I had a photo of him, one I'd taken during our first Christmas together. We hadn't had much money that first year but we'd still gotten a tree, a small one that could barely hold a handful of ornaments. For his present, I had knitted him a sweater although at the time, I wasn't much for crafts. One sleeve was longer than the other and the neck opening of the sweater was so large that it nearly hung off of one of David's shoulders. I'd been so disappointed that the sweater hadn't turned out as I'd wanted it to but David had pulled it on anyway, declaring it to be his favorite item of clothing. I'd taken a photo of him by our little tree, wearing the sweater and a huge grin on his face, and it was that photo I held to my heart most nights after his death. The picture slowly grew rumpled over time as a side effect of my falling asleep on it so many times but still, David's smile, frozen in time, endured.

The first Christmas after David's death was the hardest. Both Johnny and Heather were home with me and I tried to muster up some holiday spirit but it just felt like there was a dark, empty space where David should have been. On Christmas Eve, the three of us sat around the small living room, each of us with mugs of hot chocolate in our hands as we admired the small Christmas tree. It wasn't as small as the one from David's and my first year of marriage, but it certainly wasn't as grand as trees of Christmases past.

"Mom?" Heather finally said.

"Yeah, honey?"

"I have something to tell you," she said, looking down at her mug. It was then that I noticed she'd barely drunk any of it.

"What is it?" I asked, my anxiety rising. Was she struggling in school? Was she in some sort of trouble?

"I, um . . ." she started, faltering a little.

"Honey, what is it? You can tell me," I said gently. I glanced at Johnny but his expression was unreadable.

"I'm engaged," Heather said slowly, looking up from her mug of hot chocolate to gauge my reaction.

"You're engaged?" I asked, a smile spreading over my face.

"Yeah. It all happened so fast and I wasn't sure how you'd . . . take the news. You know, with dad and everything," she said cautiously.

"Honey, I love you and I want you to be happy, you know that," I said. "You're engaged!" I exclaimed, the news really starting to sink in. I jumped up, sloshing my hot chocolate a little on my hand as I set it on the side table before I enveloped Heather in a hug. Moments, later, I felt Johnny hugging both of us and, for just a moment, I thought I could feel David in there, too.

Heather was engaged to a lovely young man named Tim.

He was a senior at the same university Heather attended and, as I discovered when he joined us for Christmas dinner the next day, there was no one in the world he loved more than Heather. Although they'd only been dating for a few short months, they were clearly a solid match for one another. Was it soon for an engagement? Sure, but as David had taught us all, you never know how much time you have left. If Heather was happy with Tim, then I was happy for her.

Planning Heather's wedding for the following summer ended up being a good thing for me as it gave me something to focus on other than how much I missed David. There were still nights that I fell asleep with his photo clutched in my hand but on others, I found my mind swimming with color palettes and floral arrangements. During that time, I also started seeing a therapist who helped me begin to sort through my grief because I knew I was in danger of using Heather's wedding as a substitute for my focus to suppress my sadness over David and I didn't want to do that. I didn't want Heather's wedding to be a substitute for anything, I wanted it to be a happy addition. Slowly, I began to feel stronger. I still missed David, but with the help of therapy my sadness started to feel more manageable. I no longer felt like I was completely underwater and I was starting to break the surface.

Heather and Tim married on a hot day in July. The ceremony was small, just immediate family and a few friends on the beach. The ocean breeze blew in during the ceremony, whipping around our legs as the couple said their vows. I smiled as I watched them. As a parent, I think you're always worried about how well you're raising your kids, are you teaching them enough?, are you doing the right things, and so forth. But one thing I felt sure of is that as Heather promised to love Tim through better or worse, through sickness and in health, she really knew what that meant. I closed my eyes for a moment, feeling the wind and sun on my skin and for the first time since David died, I really and truly felt like I might be okay.

That fall, I returned to school to complete my Master's degree. Between working full-time and my studies, I had little time to think of anything else. I was still attending therapy and little by little, I was piecing myself back together. I hadn't forgotten about my friends from school, but in the wake of my loss of David, it was hard to miss anyone but him.

Soon after I finished my degree, Johnny moved out with his girlfriend and I realized I was on the precipice of a new chapter of my life. One Saturday morning, I was sitting in my kitchen drinking a cup of coffee when I suddenly looked around the room as if I'd never seen it before. For the first time, this place didn't really feel like home anymore. I flipped to the back of the newspaper to the classifieds and found several apartment listings. I gulped my coffee, put on my shoes, and immediately made the rounds until I found a new one bedroom apartment. It had wonderful natural light and felt so airy and open instead of sad and gray and full of painful memories like my current apartment. Plus, it was conveniently located near my new job at a guidance center. I signed a lease and returned back to my current home to begin the packing process. I had a month until I could move in, but I knew if I waited until the last minute, I'd never get everything done. However, once I returned to my apartment, I found little that I wanted to take with me. Short of some family photos and keepsakes, everything else felt like a part of my past. I bought new furniture for my new home, delicate and feminine furnishings that felt like me and a new wardrobe of bright, colorful clothes. I felt like a butterfly, finally pushing my way out of a cocoon, and I felt ready for this next part of my life. Before I left my old apartment for the last time, I took out the photo of David from our first Christmas. Instead of crying, the photo made me smile. I had no idea what had happened to that sweater, likely lost or donated years ago when the kids were little, but I still had the photo. The picture had taken some abuse over the last couple of years from all the times I'd cried and pressed it to my heart, but it still represented such a beautiful part of my life. I reflected on how lucky I'd been to have David in my life. I thought of the diner where we'd had our first date and the milkshakes from our anniversaries. I thought of summer vacations with the kids and holidays. I thought of the nights we'd spent cuddled on the couch, our fingers interlaced. I still missed him terribly but more than anything, I felt grateful to have known that kind of love. The photograph, battered and bruised though it may have been, was a symbol of how far I'd come.

"I love you, David. I always will," I said. I folded the picture and tucked it into the back of my wallet. Always in my heart, never forgotten.

Saturdays were my usual grocery shopping days. The store was often crowded, full of people like me trying to use their weekend to take care of their errands, but I'd always liked grocery shopping. There was something satisfying about filling a shopping cart--and later the fridge--with wholesome, delicious foods (and a few that weren't--I wasn't immune to ice cream's siren call). The whole process felt very regenerative to me.

One such Saturday, I was waiting in line for the cashier with my cart. I'd grown bored of scanning the tabloid headlines and my gaze drifted around the store. Striding towards the door with a bag of groceries, I saw a familiar-looking blonde woman. I examined her, unsure if I was really seeing her. I left my cart for a moment and walked over to her.

"Judy?" I asked, trying to contain my excitement. The blonde woman turned and stared at me for a moment before recognition flooded her face.

"Oh my God, Diana! Hi!" she exclaimed, immediately pulling me into a tight hug. "I can't believe it's really you!"

"Oh God, I've missed you! How are you?" I asked, so thrilled to see her. I noticed she'd lost a lot of weight, she was so thin compared to how she'd looked in school, but then I supposed I'd probably changed in the last couple of decades as well.

"I've missed you too! And I'm fine," she said, digging into her purse. I glanced back at the line and saw that the woman in front of me had kindly pulled my cart forward behind her, preserving my place in line. "I'm so sorry, but my sister is waiting for me so I can't stay," she said, scribbling something on a scrap of paper. "But this is my number--please call me! We must get together as soon as possible."

I promised I would and she left, throwing me one more brilliant smile over her shoulder. I walked back to my place in line, clutching her phone number in my hand. I felt like someone had just handed me a winning lottery ticket.

I called Judy that evening and we agreed to have dinner at my apartment on the following Friday. Over lasagna, we reminisced over old memories from school and traded stories of our lives since leaving Rosemont Academy.

"He was really handsome," Judy said, admiring the creased Christmas photo of David from my wallet before passing it back to me. I looked at the photo and smiled.

"Yeah, he was," I said. I picked up the bottle of wine we'd been sharing and Judy held out her glass for me to fill. "So, what about you?" I asked, glancing down at her bare left hand. "Did you ever marry? Have kids?"

I Love You, Not

Judy shook her head a little sadly.

"No, not yet," she said. "There have been a lot of great 'almosts', but I still haven't found my soulmate." Judy paused, taking a sip of wine. "I live with my sister and her family and they're great, but . . . I don't know. I wish I had someone of my own, you know?"

I told her that I understood.

"Are you in touch with the other girls?" I asked, taking a sip of my own wine. Judy shook her head.

"I saw Annie a few years ago by chance at a restaurant but we never got around to making plans together. And Francesca, I haven't heard from her since we left Rosemont. What about you?"

I told her that I was in the same boat, minus seeing Annie, and that she was the first of the girls I'd seen in years. Judy promised to try and dig up Annie's contact information and that we'd all get together soon. We hugged before she left, our friendship renewed, and we swore to one another that this time we wouldn't lose touch. And this time, it was a promise we'd keep.

Two weeks later, Judy called to let me know she was able to get in touch with Annie and, if I was free, they'd planned to meet at a nearby coffee shop on Sunday. However, she hadn't had any luck finding Francesca. I agreed, wishing all four of us could reunite, but I was so excited to see Annie.

On Sunday, I parked my car outside the small coffee shop and walked inside. I scanned the room, my eyes still adjusting to the cool interior from the bright California sun outside, when I heard a cry of excitement. Before I knew it, Annie had barreled into me, wrapping me in a huge hug that nearly knocked me over. For a moment, I felt transported back to high school when I'd received similar hugs from her after our soccer team had won a match. She finally released me and pointed me towards the table she already shared with Judy and, after I ordered my coffee, I joined them. In a juxtaposition to her nostalgic enthusiasm with which she greeted me, Annie had become soft-spoken over the years and she seemed too sophisticated now. She very well could have been one of the heroines in her beloved romance novels, which Annie confessed she still read often. Annie told us of her marriage to Stephen who was, in fact, not a pirate after all, but a CPA. Their three kids were now out of the nest and although Annie no longer played soccer, she was in the midst of training for her fourth triathlon.

"So how can we find Francesca?" I asked as we sipped the last of our coffees.

"I'm not sure," Judy said. "I've been trying to locate her but none of the numbers I have are still in use."

"I wonder what she's been up to," Annie mused thoughtfully.

"Maybe she's become a major star and we just don't know about it?" I asked with a sly smile and a raised eyebrow. Annie and Judy laughed.

"I suppose anything is possible," Judy said.

We said our goodbyes soon after and left with promises to meet again soon. Shortly after that Sunday, my life began to get much, much busier. After spending some time working at the guidance center, I felt I was ready to open my own practice. I decided to partner with Jack, another therapist from the guidance center, and although things were slow to start, they slowly added steam--both personally and professionally. In addition to being a wonderful business partner, Jack was kind and loving. He proposed to me twice but I hadn't been able to bring myself to say yes. Both Johnny and Heather adored Jack and encouraged me to move forward in our relationship but something still held me back. At our weekly coffee meetups,

Annie hypothesized that I felt some sort of infidelity to David to even consider the possibility of marrying someone else. Judy thought I was just scared. I wasn't sure if either of them was completely right, but I think both of them were to a certain extent. After the practice began to take off, I purchased a lovely three bedroom home and shortly after, Jack moved in with me. Part of me felt like I was giving him a consolation prize in place of actually marrying him, but Jack never complained. He understood the love I would always have for David and I knew he would patiently wait until I was ready--if I was ever ready.

The week before Christmas, I was deep in the thick of the holidays. I was still gift shopping, hanging decorations, and planning the annual Christmas party I'd started after moving into my home two years earlier. The guest list was full of Jack's and my family and friends, including Annie and Judy and their families, and while I adored the party itself, the preparations often left me feeling anxious and overwhelmed. Business was quite busy as well because while it was the most wonderful time of the year for some, it highlighted the suffering of others. Of course, I understood this from a professional standpoint as a therapist but on a personal note as well. The duality of the holidays resonated within me as well. I loved spending the time with my family, especially Heather and Tim's baby girl, but I still missed David. It was impossible to spend two decade's worth of Christmases with someone and not miss them.

Jack had taken over the responsibility of all the last minute details in the office as we prepared to close the office for Christmas and New Year's Eve so I could focus on the party preparations. I appreciated his thoughtfulness so much, highlighted by the way I walked into my office to find a steaming cup of coffee waiting for me on my desk, complete with a chocolate kiss at its side. I smiled as I unwrapped the foil and popped the chocolate into my mouth. It was 9:00 am and generally far too early in the day for candy for me, but I allowed myself to indulge in the spirit of the holidays. I flipped open my planner and began to skim through my to-do list for tomorrow night's party. I was mentally calculating the amount of wine I'd need to pick up for the event when I heard a light tap on my office door.

"Come in," I called, still studying my list. The door opened and I glanced up to see Jack, which immediately brought a smile to my face.

"Hey, you," he said, grinning at me. He had such a wonderful smile that still caused my stomach to flutter. I sometimes felt like a giddy high school girl around him, even after our years together.

"Thanks for the coffee," I said. Jack closed the door behind him and walked around to my side of the desk. He leaned down, resting a hand on each of the arm rests so that we were eye level with one another.

"What about the kiss?" he asked slyly. I leaned forward and gently pressed my lips to his.

"Thanks for that, too," I said. He kissed me again before he straightened up and walked around the desk to sit in one of the chairs to face me.

"We got an interesting call this morning," Jack said, crossing a foot over one knee.

"Oh? What sort of call?" I asked, itching to look back at my planning list.

"A woman named Alexandra. She asked for you specifically but refused to come into the office--she wants to do all of her sessions over the phone."

"That's a little unorthodox," I said, frowning.

"I know," Jack said. "She also has some restrictions. She

doesn't want to be prescribed any medications, she insists that we don't record her calls, and we can't take any notes. She also wants to do away with any time limits on her sessions and she won't schedule; she just wants to call as she sees fit."

"That's ridiculous!" I exclaimed. "I have other patients, I can't be at this woman's beck and call."

"I know," Jack said, uncrossing his legs to put both feet flat on the floor. He leaned forward, resting his elbows on his knees. "What concerns me is that she might be in some sort of dire situation. I offered to treat her myself but she insisted that it had to be you. Money doesn't seem to be an object for her and . . ." he paused. "I don't know, Diana. I think she might need some real help. You know how hard it can be for people to take that first step and ask for help. I'd hate to deter her from getting the therapy she needs."

I sighed, knowing he was right.

"Alright, fine. I'll take her on," I said. "So do we have any idea when I'm supposed to get my first mystery phone call?"

"She said she'd call back sometime today."

I groaned.

"Really, Jack? I have a hundred things to do for this party tomorrow! I was only going to be here for an hour or so to finish up before we close the office."

Jack leaned over the desk to check my list.

"Write out whatever I can pick up at the store for you," he said.

"Oh, Jack, I couldn't ask you to do that!" I said. "You've already taken on so much in getting the office ready for the break."

He responded by reaching over and pulling the page from my planner with my to-do list on it.

"Hey!" I protested but he was already walking out the door, waving at me from over his shoulder. I smiled.

I didn't have to wait long for that first call because fifteen minutes later, Jack buzzed me on my desk phone from the front desk.

"It's her," he said. I thanked him and took a moment before pushing the button to pick up the call. I felt a little annoyed by this woman's demands but Jack was right--if she was asking for help, she probably needed it. I pushed the blinking red button.

"Hello, Diana speaking," I said.

"Thank you for taking my call," a quiet voice said. There was a long pause.

"What may I call you?" I asked.

"Alexandra," the voice said quickly. "But that's not my legal name. Is that okay?"

"Sure," I said. "So, Alexandra, why don't you tell me why you've reached out to me?" Another long silence followed and I began to draw slow, frustrated circles on the notepad in front of me. "Alexandra, are you there?" I asked.

"I am very, very sad," Alexandra finally said.

"Why is that?" I asked.

She sighed somberly.

"I have a lot of reasons. I . . . I'm not sure where to start. Everything feels like a big mess."

I waited.

"I want to write you some letters. I feel like I can explain myself better that way. Is that okay?"

"Sure, that's no problem, I look forward to reading them. I'm all ears now, though, if there's something you want to talk about while we're on the phone," I said.

"Where do you want me to start?" she asked.

"Anywhere you want," I said. I was beginning to feel a little impatient but I masked it in my voice.

"I don't know. Everything is so jumbled up but I'll just say whatever comes to mind."

I turned my chair to face the window while I waited.

"All my life I've searched for love. That's 50 years of searching. You have no idea how I've longed for it. When I was younger, I got this idea in my head about what love was from the books I read or the TV shows I watched. But that all turned out to be a bunch of lies. Love was nothing like that for me."

"Alexandra, what was your childhood like?"

"Childhood," she said with a sigh. "I don't know. Normal, I guess. But then, I guess I don't have much of a basis for comparison. What's normal for me isn't necessarily normal for someone else, you know?" Alexandra paused for a long moment. "My parents loved each other. At least I thought they did. Looking back, it seems more like an obsession rather than love. They were really young when they got married and I don't really think they knew what love was. Two jealous, possessive people found one another and called it love."

"Tell me more about your mom and dad," I said, my interest piqued.

"Mom was beautiful. If you've seen a photo of Ava Gardner, you've seen my mom--she was a dead ringer. She had a fiery personality, a real wildcat. My dad was charming, handsome. Built like a marine with blue eyes and light brown hair, streaked with gold. Women couldn't resist him."

"What were they like together?" I asked. Over the phone, I listened to the flick of a cigarette lighter and a deep inhalation as she took a puff.

"They were crazy sons of bitches," she said with a dry laugh devoid of humor. "They fought like cats and dogs."

"Did the fights ever get physical?" I asked.

"No, nothing like that," Alexandra said. "Dad was all arts and music and Mom was all books and intellect. He wanted to be a musician or something but my mother forbid it."

"Why was that?" I asked.

"I don't know," she said. I could almost hear the shrug in her voice. "But I figure that was a big source of his unhappiness with her."

"It's hard to maintain a healthy relationship when one person attempts to control the other," I said. Alexandra snorted derisively.

"You can say that again," she said. Her comment reminded me of when Johnny was about four or five. It was a really windy day and as we'd tried to rush from the house to the car, he'd said, "Boy, is it windy!"

"You can say that again!" I'd said, holding his hand as we'd walked quickly.

"Boy, is it windy!" he had repeated before he'd laughed uproariously. The memory made me smile.

"Tell me more about your home life," I requested.

"Our home didn't feel like love," she said. "There was always an undercurrent of mistrust, jealousy, and unhappiness. I don't know if I ever really knew what love was. As a kid, I was always afraid of the next fight between them. After it was over, the house would be plunged into an icy silence, sometimes for days. I always felt like I was watching from a distance, waiting for some glimmer of hope to emerge. But it never did." She paused and I could hear her take another drag on her cigarette. "It seemed like they hardly ever remembered I was there. Every fight left me feeling like I'd lose my parents and I'd be left all alone, even more so than I already was. I don't know, I guess I've never really been able to shake that feeling."

"Our relationships with our parents can have a severe impact on our self-image, even well into adulthood," I said, nodding even though she couldn't see me over the phone.

"I suppressed a lot of those feelings for a long time," Alexandra said. "Eventually, I had to open that door again and face those memories and let me tell you, that was no party. It was more like a funeral march," she said. "I tried to protect my little brother from our parents' fights but there's only so much I could do. After many years, my mom finally left my dad. My dad and brother were heartbroken but I felt . . . I don't know what I felt. Relieved, maybe," she said thoughtfully. "I was relieved that something was going to change but I felt so broken from the years of being a spectator to their fights. Can a person ever really be mended once they're broken? Maybe you're the wrong person to ask since you're in the business of fixing people," she said with another dry, humorless laugh. "But I think that once you're broken, you're always broken. No medication, therapy, prayers, or anything else can fix what's been busted."

She was quiet, as if she was contemplating what she'd just said. I didn't think Alexandra really believed what she'd said about not believing a person could be fixed. If she did, why would she have called me?

"My parents, my brother, and I all struggled through the divorce and eventually we came out on the other side. Mom and Dad both moved on but my brother and I felt left behind. I don't think we've ever moved on. There's always something that pulls us back. At least, there is for me."

Alexandra faded into silence again and I waited, my attention rapt.

"I think I'll write you a letter about my childhood and

tell you more that way," she said, her voice suddenly brusque.

"Okay, thanks, Diana. I'll call you next week."

"Alexandra, I'm sorry, but our office is going to be closed until January 3rd for the holidays."

"That's nice that you're closing for the holidays. I'm sure you're going to be very busy with shopping and parties and all that," she said a little wistfully.

"Yes, I'll be busy. What about you, do you have any plans?"

"No, no plans," she said softly. "Okay, I'll talk to you soon. Merry Christmas," she added, almost as an afterthought. I opened my mouth to wish her the same but I heard the phone click in my ear as she hung up. I replaced my phone's receiver in its cradle and stared at it for a long time before I finally stood up and went to retrieve my to-do list from Jack.

The next day, I was thrilled to learn that Jack had hired outside help for the party. I had decorated the house, but Jack had taken care of the catering, servers, and bartenders. He'd seen me at Christmas parties past, running around like mad as I tried to be everywhere at once and this year, he'd given me the gift of peace. For the first time, I could really enjoy the party without worrying we'd run out of ice or that I'd forgotten a tray of hors d'oeuvres in the oven. I was looking forward to spending time with Annie and Judy, I hadn't seen them much since I became embroiled in the holiday season.

By 6:30, most of the guests had arrived except for Judy.

"Have you talked to her today?" I asked Annie as she took a sip of eggnog. Annie shook her head.

"No, but I know she's planning on coming tonight. I'm sure she just got stuck in traffic or something."

Thirty minutes later, Judy still hadn't arrived.

"Was there a message on the machine? Did she cancel?" I asked Jack.

"No message, but she did call," Jack said.

"She did? Why didn't you tell me?" I asked.

"She just said she was running behind but she was on her way, I didn't think it was necessary to get you. Besides, you were busy talking to Stephen."

I rolled my eyes.

"He was just going on and on about the upcoming tax season. I wouldn't have minded the interruption," I said. I adored Annie's husband but I didn't find the tax code nearly as fascinating as he did. Jack laughed.

"My apologies, I'll be sure to rescue you next time," he said, kissing my cheek.

Just then, the doorbell rang. I left Jack and hurried to open it. I flung open the door to find Judy.

"There you are!" I exclaimed, pulling her into a hug.

"Sorry, I got held up," she said, not sounding the least bit sorry. "Diana, I have a surprise for you."

"But you already gave me a Christmas gift," I said with a laugh. "I'm just glad you're here so the party can start."

Judy grinned but didn't say anything. Instead, she just stepped aside and gestured to the front porch. There, just outside my front door, was Francesca. I involuntarily screamed in delight and flung myself at her and she caught me in a massive hug. I heard Annie yelling from behind and suddenly she barreled into us, wrapping both of us up in her arms. The rest of the party guests, thinking something bad had happened, all clustered around the front door and watched as the four of us jumped around and squealed like hyperactive teenagers.

"Francesca, I've missed you so much," I said in her ear, still holding her tightly.

"Fran, you look amazing," Annie said. "I am so, so happy to see you!"

For the rest of the evening, I have to admit that I wasn't much of the hostess that I usually was. Instead of making the rounds through the party to mingle with all of my guests, I holed up with my three oldest friends in my bedroom as we talked, reminisced, and laughed. Jack stopped in periodically to drop off snacks and refill our drinks before winking at me and shutting the door behind him.

"So what's the story there?" Francesca asked, taking a sip of her wine as she nodded to where Jack had just stood.

"Jack is great," I said. "He's my partner in every sense of the word."

"But you're not married," Francesca said.

"Not for a lack of effort on his part," Judy interjected.

"He's asked you to marry him?" Francesca asked.

"Several times," Annie answered.

"Why haven't you said yes?" Francesca asked.

"I don't know," I said.

"She feels some latent guilt over marrying Jack, like she'd be betraying David," Annie said.

"Are you the shrink or am I?" I asked, playfully poking her in the side. Annie laughed. "Okay, enough about me," I said. "Francesca, what about you? Married? Kids? Are you an actress? Tell us everything."

"Well, I'm none of those. Single, no kids, and not an actress. But I've lived an unimaginable life," Francesca said, raising her glass in a toast. We raised our glasses as well and clinked them together.

"Tell us about it," Judy urged as we sipped our drinks.

"Later," Francesca said, reaching for another hors d'oeuvre.

"You know, Diana, I was jealous of you at school," Annie admitted.

"Jealous of me? I was jealous of you! Annie, you were the sports superstar of the school!" I exclaimed in disbelief.

"I was, wasn't I?" Annie said with a sarcastic smile and a deep sigh, as if the weight of her greatness was almost too much to bear.

"Well I'm jealous of all of you," Francesca said. "Marriages, kids, homeowners, businesses, the works. But it's a good kind of jealous," she assured us.

"I don't have any of that," Judy countered.

"You never met your soulmate?" Francesca asked, raising a sly eyebrow at her.

"No, I haven't," Judy said with a childish pout that made all of us laugh as Annie gave her a sideways hug.

"I," Annie began, straightening up with importance as she changed the subject, "have something to share about Francesca that I don't think any of you know."

"There's nothing we don't know about Francesca," Judy said dismissively.

"Oh, Judy, you can never know everything about anyone," I said.

"Oh come on, Diana, I know that. But we've known Fran forever. Sure, the last few years haven't been filled in yet, but that's forthcoming. She's never hidden anything from us," Judy said. Francesca said nothing, smiling faintly as she gazed off into space.

"Ladies, can we quit with the analysis so I can get on with my story?" Annie asked. We quieted down obediently. "Thank you."

"One day, I saw Fran standing in front of the full length mirror in the main bathroom at Rosemont. She was wearing nothing but her underwear but I was curious to see what she was going to do so I hid behind the wall and waited. After a minute or two, I heard her say, 'One day, I will be the greatest actress in the world. Women will want to be me and men will dream of me. I will be a legend, walking the red carpet in full glory and my picture will be on the cover of ever magazine. I will be like Marilyn Monroe reincarnated.'"

Everyone in the room was silent until Francesca suddenly let out a huge, barking laugh that broke the tension.

"Marilyn would be turning in her grave, what a joke that was," Francesca said, a smirk still playing on her lips.

"And then?" Judy asked impatiently.

"That's it," Annie said. "Then I left. I felt creepy, just watching her stand there in her underwear.

"You were creepy," Francesca said, playfully hitting her with one of my bed pillows.

"That's quite the ambition!"

We all turned to see Jack standing in the doorway. None of us had heard him return.

"That's how passionate Fran was about her acting and eventual rise to fame," Annie explained.

"Ladies, I don't mean to interrupt, I just wanted to check in and see how you're doing with drinks and food."

"We're fine, thanks, Jack," Judy said with a smile. He nodded to the four of us and left, closing the door once more behind him.

"So what happened to your pursuit of the red carpet?" Judy asked.

"Life, my darling. Life happened," Francesca said, a little sadly as she raised her glass again. "To life."

"To life," we echoed.

"Now, I have a story about you, Miss Annie," Judy said.

"This better be good," Annie said, settling back to listen with a challenging smile.

"Francesca was dating Alexander," Judy began.

"Alexander?" Francesca asked quietly, trying to remember. "Oh! Alexander Klein. God, he was boring."

"Anyway," Judy continued. "Francesca was dating Alexander but I guess she wasn't happy, apparently he was boring, so after about a month she broke up with him. One day, we were sitting outside on a bench by the library when Annie walked up and asked if Francesca would mind if she went out with Alexander. I wasn't sure if Francesca was going to be upset or not, but she simply shrugged and said, 'you can have him, he's not all that.'"

We all laughed.

"Wait, I'm not done," Judy said. "A week later, all the students were getting ready to go to class and we saw Annie walk in, followed shortly be Alexander. Annie's hair was all over the place and he was tucking in his shirt. Now, Annie, my question for you: what exactly where you doing?"

Annie laughed.

"As I recall, we were just rolling around on the teacher's desk. Nothing happened," she said innocently.

"You didn't find him boring like Francesca?" I asked, raising an eyebrow.

"I didn't require him to talk," Annie said and we all burst into peals of laughter.

"Did you ever 'roll on the teacher's desk' with him, Fran?" I asked. She shook her head.

"No, sweetheart," she replied. "Without a stimulating conversation, he couldn't stimulate anything else in me."

We broke into laughter again and as I giggled with my old friends, it occurred to me how happy I was to have my friends filling my home with joy.

A little later, Francesca said she needed a cigarette so we

finally left the bedroom. Annie and Judy wandered back amongst the other guests and I followed Francesca out onto the back patio.

"Do you have any regrets?" I asked her as she flicked her lighter once, twice before the flame sprang up and caught the end of her cigarette. She inhaled deeply and expelled gray smoke out of her nostrils like a thoughtful dragon.

"About not 'rolling on a desk' with Alexander? No, none," she said with a smile.

"You know what I mean," I said.

"Why, do you?" she asked. I sighed.

"Not really. Well, maybe. I wish I'd told David how I felt about him more often. He was a good man. A really good man."

"I'm sure he knew," Francesca said. "I mean, you did all you could, right?"

"Right," I said, thinking for a moment as I stared out at the large backyard behind the house. Sitting in the middle was a beautiful gazebo and, truth be told, it was a major factor in my decision to buy the house. I loved sitting out there on the weekends, reading a book or having coffee with Jack. "It's funny how we forget that love is something that we can never get enough of," I said. "We take so many things for granted and focus on so many insignificant things while forgetting that life is but a moment in time."

"You sound like a song now," Francesca said with a smile. I laughed.

"I suppose I do," I conceded. "I've missed you so much, Fran," I said, putting an arm around her. She exhaled her lungful of smoke and wrapped me in a hug.

"I've missed you too," she said. "You're the best, Diana. The best."

The evening ended with new memories and promises of

sisterhood. Now that I had my friends back, I swore to myself that I'd never let them go. Standing with Jack at the front door, waving to the last of our guests, I realized that it was possible for me to have more than one great man in my life. David, as I had told Francesca, had been a great man. But standing with Jack, at the front door of our home, I realized I was holding the arm of another great man. David and Jack didn't have to be either/or in my heart. They could be an "and."

"I love you, Jack," I said. He looked at me and smiled.

"I love you too, Diana."

Two weeks later, Jack and I walked into the office hand in hand. Our staff was already there, excitedly sharing their holiday stories. The receptionist had a funny story about a food fight that had broken out at her sister's house over dinner on Christmas Eve and one of the younger guys had a New Year's Eve story filled with hijinks and drinking stories, some of which I was sure were greatly exaggerated by the alcohol he'd consumed that night. For once, I actually had an exciting announcement of my own.

"Jack proposed to me on Christmas Day," I said. The office's conversations dropped into silence and everyone stared at me, slack jawed in anticipation. "I said yes," holding up my hand with the ring as evidence. To my surprise, even the men in the office let screams of excitement as everyone cheered. I was quickly flocked by the women who wanted to see the ring as the men shook Jack's hand and congratulated him. I thanked each of them and, finally, was able to escape to my office, where the phone was already ringing.

"This is Diana," I said when I picked up the receiver.

"Good morning. I hope you had a merry Christmas."

I sat down at my desk, my smile fading a little as Alexandra's voice brought me back to reality.

"Good morning, Alexandra. How was your Christmas?"

"I stayed home. I didn't do anything."

"Why is that?" I asked.

"My dad's in the hospital. He's very sick. Cancer, kidney failure, bowel obstruction, and the list goes on and on."

"Oh my goodness, I'm so sorry to hear that."

"That's my main source of sadness right now. I don't know, I just feel like I can't fully accept or understand it. I cry and I beg and pray to God to have mercy on my dad but nothing is happening," Alexandra said.

"Alexandra, you can't do anything about your dad's illness. It is what it is. Thinking otherwise just punishes you unnecessarily."

"He's married to this woman who does nothing but dress up, wear too much makeup, and act like the world revolves around her. It's hard to watch, you know? I'm the one who does everything for my dad. Women like her give women like us a bad name," she said. I could hear the anger in her voice.

"Maybe your dad doesn't mind her behavior. After all, he married her, he must have known what she was like."

I could hear Alexandra's exasperated sigh on the other end of the phone.

"Well at the very least, maybe she could try and take on some of the responsibilities around the house."

"Alexandra, we can't control what others do, only how we react to it."

She was quiet for a long moment.

"If I lose my dad, it will be like losing myself all over again," she said quietly.

"What do you mean by losing yourself all over again?" I asked.

"My dad and I have so many dreams to accomplish together.

I want him to walk me down the aisle, he never had a chance to do it before. I want to buy him things and take him places that he's always wanted to go but if he . . . we might never have a chance for any of that."

"I can tell he means a lot to you," I said.

"Oh absolutely, family means everything to me, especially my dad. He wasn't really around when I was a kid, but about ten years ago, we started rebuilding our relationship. And now . . . he's my best friend. He doesn't judge me and he understands me. He's a dreamer, like me. We're so much alike," Alexandra said.

"Are you married?"

"I was," she said curtly. I could hear her walls coming back up but I gently pushed forward anyway.

"What happened?"

"That's a long story."

"Can you tell me about it?"

"No," she said. "I just wanted to call and tell you that I might not be in touch for a while. My dad is back in the hospital and it's serious, really serious this time. I can't afford to be away from him for a moment."

"I understand," I said. "Don't worry about it. I'm always here for you when you're ready, Alexandra."

She was quiet for a long time. I wondered if she had hung up until she spoke suddenly.

"Would it be okay if I wrote to you?" she asked. "You can still charge me by the hour if you want."

"Of course, I told you before, you're welcome to write to me anytime," I said.

"I just need to vent this stuff out. I just feel so sad and heartbroken and I don't know if I want to cry or scream . . . if I could die instead of him, I would. I don't want to lose my dad. What would I do without him? Who would I turn to? I'd have nobody."

She paused and then suddenly an anguished scream pierced through the phone. I could hear her sobbing on the other end of the line. I waited.

"God, please don't take my dad," she begged. "But if you have to, then do it sooner rather than later. I can't stand to watch him suffer and I don't want him to be just another body in a nursing home." She sniffed and I could hear fresh tears in her voice. "Take me, God. Just don't take my dad."

For the first time in my professional career, I was speechless. I felt so powerless to help her and I just waited patiently for her to speak again, grabbing a tissue from the box on my desk to dab at the corners of my eyes. Alexandra grew quiet, her crying finally subsiding.

"I'll write to you. Thank you," she said. She hung up before I could say anything. I sat there quietly for a long time, thinking about what Alexandra had said. I imagined what it was like to be in her shoes, wiping my tears away with the scratchy tissue. It occurred to me that I really should buy better tissues, these were unnecessarily harsh on the skin. I knew the tissues were irrelevant in light of what I'd just heard, but I still couldn't help but wonder what sort of therapist has terrible tissues. The phone on my desk buzzed and I clicked the intercom button.

"Yes?"

"Diana, your next appointment is here," the receptionist said, her voice sounding slightly mechanical over the phone. I blew my nose, further disliking the tissues.

"Thank you, send him in."

The remainder of the month passed with no letters from Alexandra. This thought remained in the back of my mind and I always checked the day's mail, but there was nothing.

In the meantime, Jack and I began to plan our wedding and we decided to get married in the backyard of our home. We certainly had the space and I couldn't imagine anywhere I'd rather wed Jack than standing in the beautiful gazebo. The guest list was small, just my children and their families, Jack's sister and her family, a few colleagues from the office, and, of course, Francesca, Annie, and Judy with their families. About a week before the big day, I received a beautiful, hand engraved card from Francesca with an apology that she would be unable to attend the wedding due to a business trip, but she congratulated us all the same and promised to celebrate with us when she returned. I received the card at my office and was just closing it, feeling a little sad that Francesca wouldn't be there, when the door to my office suddenly opened, hitting the wall with a bang and causing me to jump in my chair.

"Don't you know you're not supposed to barge into a therapist's office?" I asked, placing a hand on my chest as I felt my heart rate drumming beneath it.

"Oh well, what's done is done," Annie said with a shrug as she and Judy each took a seat in front of my desk. "So, we're here to discuss something of vital importance with you."

"Oh? What's that?" I asked.

"You are getting married in a week," Annie said.

"Yes, I'm aware."

"You can't walk down the aisle naked," Annie continued.

"Well technically I suppose I could, but that might be in poor taste," I said with a grin, leaning back in my chair.

"We know you said you didn't want any help with the wedding preparations," Annie continued, ignoring me. "But we wanted to come by and offer to take you wedding dress shopping."

"Right now," Judy said.

"That's so sweet," I began, remembering an almost identical conversation I'd had with Heather the night before. "And I really appreciate the offer, but Jack and I really want to take care of all the preparations ourselves," I explained. "We just really want our guests to be able to come and enjoy the wedding, no stress."

"Told you she'd say that," Judy said to Annie, who sighed.

"I know, but we had to ask," Annie said as she smiled at me. "Can we still take you out for a bachelorette party on Friday?" she asked.

"Of course!" I said. "But we're going to behave ourselves--I mean it."

Annie rolled her eyes in faux protestation.

"Fine," she capitulated with exaggerated surrender. "But we're still going to make you wear one of those stupid sashes that says "Bride to be" and a tiara with a veil attached to it."

I laughed.

"That sounds fair," I said. Then, in a flurry of hugs and a chorus of "see you soons", they were gone.

On the day of the wedding, I awoke with a slight headache. Annie and Judy had convinced me to have more drinks than I usually would have and I had a vague recollection of karaoke that I tried not to think about too much. I checked the clock on my nightstand and saw that it was nearly 11:00. Jack must have turned off my alarm to let me sleep. I smiled at the thought of him. I took a shower, allowing myself to indulge in the spa-quality soaps and lotions Annie and Judy had given me as a gift the night before, before I dressed and headed downstairs to help Jack with the final preparations before the wedding that evening. However, I discovered that everything was already taken care of. The kitchen was full of caterers and delicious smells, chairs were being set up on the back lawn, and Jack was orchestrating everything. He noticed me and smiled while he finished giving instructions to a workman.

"Good morning, darling," he said, coming over to kiss my cheek.

"Good morning, yourself," I said, looking around. "I was coming to check on the preparations to see what I could do to help but everything seems to be under control."

"You don't have to worry about a thing," Jack said. "I've got it all taken care of."

At that moment, a delivery guy walked by carrying a massive vase of ivory roses."

"Oh my God, are those for us?" I asked, gaping as more vases of the same were brought through the house and out to the backyard. Ivory roses spilled out of the gazebo, overflowing in the most romantic arrangements.

"They're from Francesca," Jack said.

"They must have cost her a fortune!" I exclaimed.

"I split the cost with her," Jack said with a humble shrug of his shoulders. "But she really wanted to do something nice for you since she couldn't be here today."

I walked closer to the window for a better view of the gazebo.

"How did she know to get ivory roses?" I asked.

"She called me a few days ago, she wanted them to match your dress. Something about you being as beautiful as a rose," he said, coming up behind me to wrap an arm around my waist.

"They're absolutely breathtaking, I couldn't have ever imagined something like this," I said, placing my hand on his. "Thank you, Jack," I said, glancing up at him. He said nothing but instead, just kissed me.

Later that afternoon, as I was getting ready, I had

commandeered the master bedroom for my preparations. I was wearing my robe and I'd just finished setting my hair and was dusting the last bit of powder on my nose when I heard a gentle knock at the bedroom door.

"Come in," I called, leaning closer to the mirror. The door opened and Jack slipped inside.

"I was hoping to catch you before you put on your dress," Jack said.

"Mission accomplished, I was just about to put it on," I said. I noticed a blue velvet box in his hand. "What's that?"

"This is from me to you," he said, holding the box out to me. He looked almost shy for a moment as I smiled, accepting the box. I opened it to find a delicate strand of pearls.

"It's so beautiful," I breathed. "Thank you, Jack."

"I was thinking," Jack said, taking the necklace from me so he could clasp it around my neck, "that you have those beautiful pearl earrings, the ones from David."

I nodded, thinking of the earrings David had given me for our tenth wedding anniversary.

"So," Jack continued, "I thought that you could wear David on your ears and me around your beautiful neck," he said as the necklace clasp clicked into place.

"This is incredible," I said. "You're incredible," I added before kissing him. He gently held my chin, tilting it up to him as we kissed.

"I'll see you out there," he said with a grin. He lightly kissed me once more before he left the bedroom. I took David's earrings out of my jewelry box and hooked them in my ears. I looked in the mirror, admiring the way Jack's pearls perfectly complimented David's, and smiled.

That evening, as the sun set and our loved ones looked on, Jack and I vowed to love one another in good times and in bad, in sickness and in health, for richer or poorer, until death did we part. Then, as instructed, Jack kissed his bride. Standing with my new husband, surrounded by our loved ones and Francesca's flowers, I knew I was one of the lucky ones.

It wasn't until May that I received my first letter from Alexandra. When the receptionist handed me my mail, part of me wanted to rip open the letter and devour it immediately, but instead, I waited. It had taken her months to write and send this letter and I wanted to give it the attention it deserved. Once my appointments were finished for the day, I told Jack I was taking off early and I drove home to our house. Once inside, I curled up in my favorite armchair, opened Alexandra's letter, and began to read.

Dear Diana,

This is my first letter and honestly, I don't know why I'm writing to you. Maybe it's a way for me to confess without questions or judgement or advice. Even though I know questions and advice are your job. I don't know, this seems easier somehow.

My dad is home and recovering well from a bowel obstruction surgery. He seems better and I hope he stays that way.

You asked me why I'm so sad. It's hard for me to say over the phone, but I can tell you part of it now. Other than watching my father suffer so much, I think most of my sadness stems from my life. The choices I've made. Immediately after I finished school, I started working for an international shipping company. There, I met a man. He was one of my two bosses but it was love at first sight. I was only 19, barely an adult at all, but I was in love all the same.

His name was Albert and he was the most beautiful thing I'd ever seen. German, with golden blond hair, piercing blue eyes, beautiful lips and face, athletic, tall, broad shoulders, and charismatic. He seemed so perfect, like I'd ordered him from a catalog or something. He had such a commanding presence and a very serious nature. He was 26 and my knees felt like Jell-O around him. The sound of his voice melted my reality, I couldn't focus on anything when he was around. I tried my best to keep my cool but I knew I failed miserably, everyone in the office could see how I felt about him. At first, Albert didn't seem to return my feelings and he used to gently tease me about my lack of work ethics, but I didn't mind. I felt like I was in heaven around him and nothing else mattered.

As time went on, he started to look at me a little differently. Staring, really. I was so infatuated with him but his staring unnerved me a little. He knew the kind of effect he had on me and he didn't stop looking at me like that. While his stares made me nervous, I wanted so desperately for him to love me like I loved him, but I never knew what was going on in his head.

One day, I poked my head into Albert's office to say goodbye for the day as I usually did and out of nowhere, he invited me over to his place. I said yes without hesitation. Once at his house, we hung out and talked. It was so nice to just be with each other outside of the office and when the evening turned into night, he kissed me. Our kisses grew more passionate and we moved to his bedroom we fooled around on his bed and I wanted him, but I was scared. I told him I was a virgin and he immediately backed off, respecting that I wasn't ready yet. Albert was such a gentleman.

As time went on I fell deeper and deeper in love with him. But then one day, he told me that he had to leave and return to Germany. I was devastated. Before he left, I wrote him a letter, begging him not to forget me and to come back to me as soon as he could. I included a photo of myself, I didn't think he had one already. He promised he would come back and before he left, he kissed me one last time.

That was the last I saw or heard from him. I forgot to include an address or phone number with my letter and we lost touch. I was never quite the same after he left. I felt like I wanted to get revenge on him for not loving me enough to find me and overnight, I changed from this nice, wholesome girl into an angry wild child. I quit my job, travelled (but not to Germany), and blew through all of my savings. I didn't care about anything but trying to have fun. I changed boyfriends like I changed my clothes, never letting anyone get too close. I never had sex with any of them; my way of lashing out at Albert was to string men along and then break their hearts as quickly as I could. I threw away a lot of good men and instead, chose to keep the bad boys around me. I was good at my game, but I was never happy.

After two years of playing this game, I finally started to grow tired of it. I watched my girlfriends get married and settle into their lives and I started to yearn for a life like that of my own. As I said, through all of my game playing, I'd remained a virgin. I wanted to *wait until I got married so I had something beautiful to offer my husband, something that I hadn't even given to Albert.*

One night, I was in London visiting some friends. It was a cold winter's night and we'd gone to a late movie. My friends lived a good ways away from the theater so when the movie ended, I decided to use the bathroom one last time. My friends waited for me and I walked into the seemingly empty bathroom. But before I could even enter a stall, a man I didn't know grabbed me by the neck and forced me on to the floor, my head painfully hitting the tiles. Before I could even try to scream, he covered my mouth with his other hand. I struggled as hard as I could but it was no use, I was too disoriented from hitting my head on the floor when he forced me down. I don't remember the man's face, I think I blacked out at one point, but I do remember how cold the tile floor was. Looking back, it seems so strange to me how memory works. I can't remember the face of the man who violated and raped me, the man who took away the one thing that was still mine. But I do remember the cold tile floor, the small spot of water that seeped into the left sleeve of my shirt as I lay on the ground.

I must have passed out because when I opened my eyes, I was still on the floor and the man was gone. I struggled to stand, the back of my head throbbing, and ended up crawling over to the sinks. I slowly pulled myself up, bracing myself on the sink, and looked up at my reflection. As soon as my eyes met those of my reflection, I choked and vomited into the clean white sink. I didn't recognize myself. I cleaned myself up as best I could, trying to make myself look normal, and left the bathroom. My friends were waiting for me outside the movie theater and I deflected the chorus of "where were yous" as best I could. We started bar hopping and by the end of the night, I don't think any of them even saw the bruises on my face because they were so drunk.

Later that night, as I lay alone in my bed, aching and hurt, I swore to myself that I would never tell anyone about the rape. Everyone knew my reputation for changing men so quickly, who would believe me? I think they all assumed I slept with all of my men anyway so a rape felt impossible to prove. That night, and in the many that followed, I cried, my heart engulfed in pain. I cursed Albert, sometimes screaming his name at the top of my lungs while I cried and begged him to come back and save me. I hated him for leaving but more than anything I missed him desperately. None of this would have happened had he come back for me, I was sure of it.

A few months later, I met a man named Andy. He was very good looking, although he was nothing like Albert. Andy was soft spoken and shy, very quiet, an artist. He pursued me for three months and I resisted, not sure I wanted to date anyone yet, but eventually I gave in. He professed his love for me and after just a few months together, he asked for my hand in marriage. However, I was nervous--I hadn't yet told him about the rape but if we were going to get married, I didn't want there to be any secrets between us. So one afternoon, I sat Andy down and I told him my story, the whole thing from start to finish.

I'm not sure what I expected, but he just dismissed the incident.

"I love you. You're safe with me," Andy assured me. I really wanted to believe him.

Once I accepted his proposal, we moved in together to help save money for the wedding. Time went on and I changed jobs to a better position, a full-time, better paying job but Andy remained unemployed. I knew how passionate he was about his art but there were still bills to pay and a wedding to save for and it seemed like he wasn't even trying to look for a job. Andy had also begun to evolve into a man I didn't recognize. He grew jealous and extremely possessive of me but, being young and naive, I just thought he loved me.

One day, while I was at work, I looked out the second floor office window to see Andy standing across the street. Surprised, I hurried downstairs and out to the sidewalk.

"Is everything okay?" I asked.

"You have to quit," he said, his eyes dark.

"What do you mean I have to quit? We need the money," I said, confused. Andy said nothing but instead grabbed me by the arm and marched me across the street and into my boss's office. Stunned and a little frightened, I did as Andy told me to and I never set foot in that office again.

Later, in our bedroom at home, I tried to ask Andy why he had done that, why he'd made me quit. He replied by punching me in the face before he threw me on our bed. I tried to fight him off but he took off his belt and started to beat me with it, the leather strap biting into my skin. I cried and begged him to stop but he didn't seem to hear me. Finally, he dropped the belt on the floor and left the room. I lay in a heap on our bed, sobbing, but he wasn't done with me. He returned shortly with a pair of gleaming silver scissors. He grabbed me by my ponytail and cut it off, throwing the hair in my face before he punched me in the side of the head and I fell to the floor. I lay there, unable to move, as I watched him take the scissors to my clothes, my books, everything that was mine. My head throbbed and my body felt like it was on fire where he'd hit me with his belt and all I had the strength to do was let the tears fall down my face. When he was done, he dropped the scissors to the floor where they landed with a clatter.

"Clean up, bitch," he said. He turned to go but suddenly whirled around and delivered a strong kick to my gut. I think I cried out but I don't know for sure. All I remember is that everything hurt.

I don't know how long I lay on the floor but eventually, I slowly pushed myself up on all fours and began to pick up the mess. My hands shook as I tried to push the scraps of paper and fabric that were once my books and clothes into a pile, figuring I would get a trash bag later. When I was able to stand, I walked to the bathroom and looked at myself in the mirror. My face was unrecognizable, swollen and bloody with purpling bruises all across it. I couldn't cry anymore, I'd left all the tears I had on the bedroom floor. I cleaned myself up the best I could and took all the trash out to the bin. Andy wasn't there, I didn't know where he was, but I hoped he'd never come back. Later, I crawled into bed as carefully as I could, my body still in immense pain. My head still hurt and I couldn't think clearly but I lay there and prayed for death. But death was not that kind to me.

Much later that night, Andy came back a very different man than he had been earlier. He lay on the bed beside me and cried, gently holding my broken body as he begged for forgiveness.

"I'm so sorry, please forgive me," he whispered. "I don't know what came over me, I promise this will never happen again. I love you, you're my whole life. I'm so, so sorry," he said. I stared at him through eyes half swollen shut.

"Why did you do this?" I asked quietly.

"I thought you were having an affair with someone at your job," he explained. "It drove me crazy to think of you with someone else."

"I wasn't," I told him. "I would never do that to you."

"Please, please forgive me," he begged.

I forgave Andy because I wanted his promises to be true. But they weren't. Of course they weren't.

A couple of months later, I discovered I was pregnant. I was so thrilled, so excited at the idea of being a mother. I jubilantly told Andy, but he didn't share my enthusiasm. He sulked around our home, muttering about how we didn't have enough money to raise a child. But I didn't let him dull my happiness. I ate as best I could despite my horrible morning sickness, I took daily walks, and I'd put headphones on my belly and played Mozart for the baby every day. I read that Mozart makes babies smarter. Each day, I'd lay in bed and talk to my belly and I already had names picked out: Natalie for a girl and Andrew James for a boy.

But things only got worse with Andy. He still hit me regularly and at least once a month, he'd fly into a rage like he had the day he made me quit my job. He didn't seem to care that I was pregnant. During one of those rages, he kicked me in the stomach and I passed out. When I awoke, I was lying in a sticky puddle of my own blood.

After I lost my baby, I fell into a deep depression. I'd cry for hours but I didn't tell anyone about my pain. I couldn't.

Once, when I was crying on our bed, Andy stormed into the bedroom, the door hitting the wall with a loud crack. He accused me of touching his paints and I tried to explain that I hadn't meant to, it was an accident, I was just trying to clean up and I bumped them by mistake. He wouldn't hear of it, didn't care about my explanation, and he started beating me, punching my torso and face. When he was winding up for another hit, I grabbed the flowerpot on the bedside table and smashed it into the side of his head. It shattered and fragments of pottery and flower petals flew everywhere. Andy slumped to the floor. I don't know if he was unconscious or dead and I didn't bother to check. I grabbed my purse and ran out, taking nothing but the clothes on my back.

When I reflect on this chapter in my life, I find it somewhat odd that I was so physically hurt by this monster masquerading as a man but emotionally, I didn't feel any pain from him. I was devastated at the loss of my baby, but that was for the baby--not *for Andy. Was it because of my young age? Was it because I never really loved him? Or was it because my head was always in a world full of dreams yet to accomplish and, on some level, I was still waiting for Albert to return? I don't know. I still don't know to this day.*

So, do you think this is enough of a reason to be sad?

Alexandra

When I finished the letter, I folded it carefully and tucked it back into the envelope. My cheeks were wet; I hadn't realized I'd been crying. I stayed in the armchair for a long time, holding Alexandra's letter to my heart.

Weeks went by and I didn't hear from Alexandra.

"Jack, what if something's happened?" I asked. "What if she's hurt herself?"

"We've seen this before," he reminded me gently. "If she's sharing her stories like this, I don't think she's going to do anything rash or irreversible."

"But, Jack, what if you're wrong? What if the pain gets to be too much and she sees no other way out?" I asked. "It happens every day."

"What do you want to do? Do you want to try and track her down?"

"No. I don't know. I wish I knew what to do," I said.

"I think all you can do is wait," Jack said. "I think she'll reach out when she's ready."

I nodded my head absently in agreement, my thoughts lost as I remembered her letter. I prayed for her each time I thought about her. It was better than doing nothing, I supposed.

About a week after my conversation with Jack, I received another letter from Alexandra. I didn't know what I'd find inside but I knew I couldn't wait until I drove home to read it so I told my receptionist to hold all my calls and quickly tore open the envelope. Inside was a letter with a small yellow note attached. The note said, "My father is back in the hospital and he's getting a blood transfusion for his leukemia. Please pray for him."

"I will," I promised aloud, my voice sounding small in my office. I set the note aside and began to read her letter.

After I left Andy, I avoided men altogether. I reveled in my singlehood, grateful for my freedom. My wild days were officially gone and I became a homebody. I found I enjoyed the solitude and I whittled down my friends to only a key few with whom I felt I truly wanted to keep in touch. I worked hard at my new job and I saved a lot of my money (a perk of staying in all the time). I read countless books, started volunteering at a local animal shelter, and discovered my love of photography. Throughout all this, I still found myself thinking of Albert. He almost never left my mind but the burning desire for his return that I'd once had had faded.

About a year later, one of the few friends I'd kept up with invited me to a party. There, I met Jon. He was Canadian, charming, and educated, so refined. He was tall, dark, and handsome, such a contrast from Albert, my golden boy. Jon and I immediately hit it off and I found I enjoyed talking with him. We had a lot in common, specifically in the arts. He was a wonderful painter and held a Master's degree in music and we enjoyed many of the same books. We discussed and debated our favorites, each challenging the other. We also shared a sense of spirituality, although he ascribed to Hinduism whereas I'm more of a Jesus person, but without all the organized stuff. I felt so mentally stimulated by him and I enjoyed our conversations immensely.

Jon was in town on a business trip but we kept in touch when he left to return to Canada. He called me every night and we spent at least two or three hours on the phone, talking and laughing. After a couple of months, we agreed for Jon to come stay with me for a month, sort of a trial run. If the month went well, he would move to the States to be with me and we would get married. I felt that I loved him and I hadn't loved anyone for a very long time.

He arrived on April 1st and we were both so excited for our trial month. I introduced him around to my family and friends. However, no one was impressed by him and I found this odd. He was courteous and friendly but my family and friends kept voicing concerns that he only wanted to be with me to get a green card. Their comments frustrated me but they also planted a little doubt in the back of my mind. I brought up the subject with Jon but he laughed it off.

"Darling, my company can get me a green card anytime," he said. "I'm with you because I love you."

I relaxed, feeling comforted by his words. I told myself that my friends and family were just being paranoid, that they just didn't know Jon like I did. The month went exceptionally well and we made plans to go forward with his move to the U.S. On

September 15th, Jon proposed to me with a gold ring studded with diamonds. I loved the diamonds but I wasn't impressed by the gold. It seemed silly to me because it was just a ring so I said nothing about the gold and instead told Jon that I, of course, would marry him. We set a date for December 10th and I planned the whole wedding myself. I wanted to create something memorable and beautiful and I managed to do it on a shoestring budget. Each of our 250 guests thought we'd spent ten times what I actually spent on the wedding because the reception was so extravagant. I wore a dress that looked just like something out of Vera Wang's line, but I found it for a deep, deep discount, ensuring I would look like a million dollars without having to spend a million dollars. I still have a photo of myself in that dress, complete with the veil, gloves, and shoes. The night of the wedding was one of the few happy nights of my life.

We didn't go on a honeymoon, but that was okay because I had to go back to work. But I told myself that this way, we could save up for a better, more romantic trip together in the future. In the meantime, Jon and I settled into our one bedroom apartment and adopted a cat, who became my joy. After about a year, I started presenting the idea of buying a house but each time I mentioned it, he would dismiss the conversation. He claimed we didn't need a house yet, that the apartment was fine, and when I'd try to argue that buying a house would be a good investment, Jon would escalate the situation into a fight, saying horribly mean things or rehashing old, forgotten arguments. Eventually, I stopped bringing it up just to avoid the fights.

Then Jon started talking about having a baby. I had told him about what happened with Andy and that I wasn't sure I was prepared to go through another pregnancy, but Jon insisted. I gave in and consulted my gynecologist. She told me that I only had a short window of opportunity to get pregnant because I was premenopausal. But then she ran some more tests, just to get a complete picture of my health, and found that my tubes were blocked. She told me that getting pregnant without assistance wouldn't be possible but we could try in vitro fertilization. I wasn't looking forward to presenting this idea to John and, as I'd expected, he vehemently rejected it.

Life went on, but Jon and I had devolved into roommates. There was no intimacy, no attraction between us. Sometimes I wondered if there ever really had been intimacy between us and if so, where had it gone? When did we lose it? It couldn't have just been about not having a baby, things weren't good long before that. Where did it all go wrong?

I tried to reach out to Jon but he rejected me at every turn. He'd taken to yelling at me, screaming profanities and insults. "You're a desert!" he'd shout. "You can't have children, you're not a woman, you skinny bitch." Or he'd say things like, "Why don't you gain some weight? Then I wouldn't have to lust after women with big asses, you stupid stick insect." If I ever tried to protest anything he said, he'd dismiss me and insist that I didn't know anything and I was stupid. "Get your degree and then you can talk to me."

I felt broken and helpless. To please him, I started drinking 5-6 Ensures a day to gain weight and I enrolled in some night classes. But nothing I did seem to impress him or change his attitude towards me. Nothing I did was ever good enough. Finally, after three years of verbal and emotional abuse, I had a breakdown in the office at my job. I was taken to the hospital and referred to a psychiatrist. I ended up losing my job but I did seek help and was ultimately diagnosed with General Anxiety Disorder and depression. I had no idea what either of those meant and I didn't really care. All I knew was that I felt like I was underwater, drowning all the time under the weight of my hopelessness. I was prescribed various medications but they made me feel like a zombie; I wasn't myself.

Throughout all this, Jon seemed to be doing well. He was happy and thriving and didn't seem to acknowledge or even notice my pain. We had applied for his citizenship before we married and he promised that once all of that was done, we could apply for dual citizenship for me with Canada. Then we could travel freely and finally go on that long forgotten honeymoon we had never taken.

For all of my adult life, my weight had been around 115lbs but now I weighed 134lbs. I forced myself to drink the Ensures and eat to try to keep my weight up to please Jon, although he never really seemed pleased by my efforts. In fact, as time went on he seemed to grow increasingly irritated with me and he picked fights over the smallest things, like forgetting to change a light bulb or taking the car to the wrong car wash.

None of the medications seemed to be working for me. My anxiety was still high and often resulted in panic attacks that would incapacitate me while my depression stayed stagnant and deep. At last, I finally found a psychiatrist with whom I was comfortable. He lowered the dosage on the pills, somewhat removing that zombie feeling, and he insisted I begin therapy as well. I agreed, on the condition that I could do my counseling with him. With this, a new chapter began in the midst of my hellish marriage. My doctor encouraged me to get out into nature and take walks, as well as write about my pain and my feelings, anything that came to mind. And so, I went to a nearby park, wrote in a journal and cried for hours each day, rain or shine.

By this time, Jon and I hardly ever talked. He lived his life and did whatever he wanted with whomever he wanted while I struggled by with my pain. And yet, in spite of all this, I still held on to hope that things between Jon and me could get better. On several occasions, I brought up the idea of seeing a marriage counselor but he always shut me down.

"I'm not going to waste time and money to have some idiot tell me how to live my life," he'd say, closing the subject. Eventually, I gave up.

One day, while Jon was out (who knows where he was), I got a call from a friend inviting me to her house. It had been ages since we'd spent time together and I accepted the invitation with enthusiasm. I put on a dress I'd once loved, blue and flowy, and heels.

When was the last time I'd worn heels? I turned to the large mirror in the bedroom to examine my reflection but I didn't see myself. I saw a stranger, someone I never could have recognized, and I felt something give way inside of me. I crumpled to the floor and cried, hugging my knees to my chest until my tears ran dry and my hiccupping sobs faded. The cat came into the bedroom and curled beside me on the floor, his warm purrs soothing me. I pushed myself up and undressed, the dress puddling on the floor as I slowly kicked off the shoes. I never made it to my friend's house, but I did manage as far as the shower. When you're drowning in depression, a shower can feel like a monumental victory. I turned on the water and after a few minutes, the bathroom began to warm as it filled with steam. I looked at the foggy bathroom mirror and saw myself clearer than I had in years. I had become a broken, hopeless woman incapable of helping herself, living at the mercy of a husband who was trying to kill whatever small bits of joy I still had within me.

I stepped into the shower and enjoyed the warm water washing over my skin. As I lathered shampoo in my hair, I heard Jon's words in my head. "You're nothing, you're worthless, nobody loves you, you're not a woman, you're a sick, crazy bitch." These words had become my inner monologue, my mantras for so long that at times I found his words indistinguishable from my own thoughts. But as I rinsed the shampoo from my hair, I felt Jon's words fading away, swirling down the drain like the useless suds.

Before Jon, I had worked hard to become a confident woman who fought for what I wanted and

believed in the beauty of people and life, but now . . .
I was barely a shadow of the person I had once been.
As I turned off the shower, I realized that I didn't
want to die. I wanted to rejoin my life and find myself
again although, after so many years of feeling lost, I
no longer knew who I was anymore or even where to
start looking.

Later that night as I lay in bed, listening to
Jon's soft snoring, I kept thinking of something my
psychiatrist had said to me: "You know what's holding
you back, but you don't want to accept it. Once you
do, you will see change." But what was holding me
back? I wasn't sure, but I had to find out. Over the
past four months, I had filled five notebooks with all
of my pain and suffering. I crept out of bed, careful
not to wake Jon, and took my notebooks to the living
room. Like a hungry wolf, I devoured my words and
felt something stirring in me, like when you have a
word on the tip of your tongue but you can't quite
remember what it is. Then, around 5:00 AM, I
found my answer.

The next day I had an appointment with my
psychiatrist and I told him what I'd discovered.

"It's my fear," I said. "It's fear that's holding me
back. I have believed every single lie Jon has told me
about being worthless or stupid or less than a woman
and I am none of those things."

"Who are you then?" the psychiatrist asked. I
looked into his blue eyes and for a moment, I saw
Albert again. "Who are you?" he repeated.

"I am a person of value," I said. Then I burst into tears. The doctor was patient and waited until I was done.

"Now what do I do?" I asked.

"Now your new life can begin," he said. I smiled.

"You're smiling, that's a good sign. I'm not sure if I've ever seen you smile. I think you're on your way, taking this first step."

When I left his office that day, I was still smiling. I went to the park near my apartment, the one that had been the site of so many scribbled notebook pages and tears. But that day, I didn't have my notebook with me. I was all by myself. I sat on my favorite bench and looked around the park, really looked around, maybe for the first time ever. Nearby, a large oak tree towered over me and the afternoon sunlight peeked through the leaves, dappling the green grass. A slight breeze blew through the park and brushed my cheek and for the first time in a very long time, I felt like I might be okay.

Within a few months and under the guidance of my psychiatrist, I was able to wean off of the antidepressants and my anti-anxiety medication was only taken as needed. I started going for long walks and making new plans. I started to lose the extra weight I'd gained in a pathetic attempt to please Jon and found a new job. I slowly tried to rebuild my credit, largely destroyed by Jon as he'd built up his own. After about a year, I found a new apartment, although I hadn't yet told Jon. On the day I signed the lease, I came home to find Jon's green card in the mailbox. Finally, after all this time. Jon was home, sitting on the living room couch when I walked into our apartment.

"I have two things to tell you," I said without hesitation.

"Okay," he said slowly, unsure of where this was heading.

"The first is that I'm leaving you. I found an apartment and I'm moving out. Tonight."

His eyes welled with tears.

"What? An apartment?" he asked. "How can you do that? I love you, I've done everything I possibly can to make you happy. I can't lose you," he said, the last of his words dissolving into tears. I sat there, a little shocked by the outpouring of emotion. I felt a little sorry for him but I felt resolute in my decision to leave.

"The second thing I have to tell you is that your green card came in the mail today," I said, handing over the envelope. His tears stopped almost immediately. He took the envelope from me and looked inside, reading the letter. His face broke into a grin. I left him on the couch and went into our bedroom, my former bedroom, and started to pack my clothes.

"I guess I can't hold you back," I heard him call from the living room. "If you want to leave, then you should. It's a free country."

I shook my head and continued packing, feeling even surer in my decision. And although this felt like the right thing to do, part of me felt that by leaving Jon, I was leaving any hope I ever had for love and a family. Later that night, when I sat on the floor of my new, empty apartment with the cat in my arms,

I realized that even if I had stayed with Jon, love and a family would never happen there either. As the cat affectionately butted its head against my chin, I thanked God for my life, thanked Him for every pain I had experienced and every tear I had shed that had brought me to this new, stronger place in my life. And for the first time in a long time, I did not cry.

Alexandra

I finished her letter and set it down gently on my desk. Alexandra might not have been crying, but I was.

More time passed without a call or letter from Alexandra until the first week of June. The day was warm and I enjoyed the late afternoon sun that shone through my office window. The air conditioning in the office was always turned down far too low for my taste so I liked the reprieve the sun brought me. My reverie was interrupted by a buzz from my receptionist, telling me I had a phone call, someone named Alexandra. I picked it up immediately.

"Good afternoon, Alexandra," I said.

"He's gone," she sobbed. "Gone forever. I'll never see him again. Never." She let out a painful cry which sent a chill down my spine, one I was sure wasn't from the overpowering air conditioning.

"Alexandra, what happened?" I asked, although I was pretty sure I already knew the answer. She sobbed until she was able to regain her composure enough to speak.

"My father died," she finally said.

"I'm so sorry," I said, meaning it.

"What am I going to do?" she wailed. "I'm lost without him. I'm dead without him. He was my best friend, the only person I could ever truly count on. Who is going to take care of me when I'm lost and confused? Who is going to comfort me and let me know that everything is going to be okay? I'll tell you who--nobody. I have no one." At this, she broke into fresh sobs.

"Alexandra, I'm so sorry," I said again, unsure of what else to say.

"I was there when he died," she said. "He looked like he was in pain but the hospital staff kept insisting that he wasn't, that he was peaceful."

This time I stayed quiet, waiting for her to say what she needed to say.

"I just wanted you to know." Alexandra said. "I'll talk to you soon."

Without waiting for my reply, she hung up. When I set down the phone I burst into tears too, surprising myself with this outpouring of emotion. I couldn't help but think of David then, how I hadn't been there when he'd died. I had no idea if David had been in pain or at peace.

Jack must have heard me crying because he rushed into my office.

"Diana, what's wrong?" he asked, hurrying around to my side of the desk. He knelt in front of me, taking my hands in his.

"Alexandra just called," I said, my breath hitching as I tried to speak. "Her father died. She was crying. You should have . . . you should have heard her crying. There was so much pain in her voice."

Jack took me in his arms, hugging me tightly.

"I know it's hard," he whispered in my ear. "You're so empathetic. It's one of the things I love most about you. But you can't take on your patients' pain. You'll break if you do and I need you."

I nodded, knowing he was right. He released me from the hug and took a tissue from the box on my desk. He dabbed the tears away from my cheeks.

"Are you okay?" he asked. I nodded again. He gave me a smile and a kiss on the forehead before he left my office, quietly shutting the door behind him. I took another tissue and blew my nose, forcing myself to regain my composure. I checked the time and, realizing I had another client arriving soon, I pulled a small mirror out of my purse and fixed my makeup, erasing any telltale signs of crying from my face.

Two months later, I received another letter from Alexandra.

My father didn't have a funeral, his wife cremated him. There was no memorial and there's no tombstone for me to visit when I miss him. I don't even have his watch or anything else of his (his wife's doing, of course). But my dad didn't like arguments, so I didn't fight her for it. He always told me to let people do what they want and try to maintain peace with everyone, so that's what I'm doing. It's what he would have wanted.

I'm doing better though. Memories of my father will last a lifetime and although I still cry for him from time to time, I think that's okay. Through it all, I'm glad my father is in a better place and he isn't suffering anymore, and I'm just moving forward one day at a time. This past year while my father endured so much pain, I feel like I learned a lot from it all. He taught me lessons that no book could have and now that I've had some time to process it, I think my father's death has given me some closure on my past. His sickness and death have helped to reintroduce me to myself.

All my life, I've looked for love in all the wrong places. All the desires I had for finding love were rooted in the love I'd longed for as a child. I thought marriage would give me everything I never had but I was wrong. Very wrong. I blamed everything and everyone for my unhappiness--and for good reason, in some cases--but this last year of watching my dad really showed me what I couldn't see before. Through his pain, he showed me the love and attention I'd longed for my whole life. He gave me back what I'd lost years ago and his suffering enabled me to see myself for who I really am and the world around me more clearly. I feel like I've found myself again.

I realize now that not everyone is cut out to be married or have a family or this idea of a storybook romance, something I thought I had to have if I was to be "normal" like everyone else. My heart was shattered when I watched my dad deteriorate in front of me but through it all, he taught me about strength, resilience, patience, forgiveness, and kindness. He gave me life before he lost his.

Thank you for everything.

Alexandra

As I put down the letter, I wished I could see Alexandra and talk to her face to face. It eased my mind a little to know that she was doing better than she had been during her last phone call, but still I worried about her. I knew that Jack was right, that I was getting too emotionally invested in my patient, but

I couldn't help it. Although we'd never met, I felt like I really connected to Alexandra. Her pain was my pain, her suffering was my suffering. And so I waited, hoping the phone would ring or a letter would arrive and then two months later, one finally came.

Leaving my husband was not the beginning of a life of freedom for me. I was off the antidepressants, but Pandora's Box was already open and I felt too exposed to the emotions and fears I'd tried to suppress for so long. It's amazing how we can go on with our lives, focusing on such mundane trivialities, and all the while forget who we really are. But now, instead of ignoring these feelings, I was determined to learn from them and understand them, especially the ones that I had no idea how to handle.

My unblocking began with one question: why do I keep going back to the past? I started reading self-help books on fear, anxiety, insecurity, personal growth, and more. I read whatever I thought could give me some insight into my own head. Some books helped, others didn't, but I made sure to keep pushing forward. I also started spending a lot of time with God, asking for help and guidance to find my answers, and to find peace within.

My life had become routine. Go to work, go home, eat something, play with the cat, and then go to bed where I'd cover my face with pillows and scream and cry until my throat was hoarse. After that I'd lie there, feeling sorry for myself while I waited for the answer to magically appear. During this time, I didn't socialize much. Spending time with others didn't really interest me, it seemed more important to stay home and keep pushing forward in my quest to unblock myself. I longed for happiness and freedom, freedom from my past, freedom from my pain. I dreamed of a life without the chains that bound me to my suffering.

Over time, I began to have breakthroughs and with each breakthrough, I created a ritual for myself. One of my first breakthroughs was the day I realized I'd made it through the pain of divorce and it no longer hurt to think of Jon. I tore the pages from the notebooks I'd filled in the park and burned them while I said a silent prayer, releasing them from my life. I started to reach out to friends again and I shared the story of my divorce with them. I expected the retelling to bring up painful emotions but instead, I felt like I was recounting a story I'd read in a book. There were no tears, no feelings, just a statement of what had happened. I celebrated this victory with a new pair of shoes and a massage--in unblocking myself, I was learning to love myself and I tried to show myself that love.

From time to time, I felt my old anxiety begin to creep in but instead of resorting to my usual medication, I found valerian root. The guy at the store said that 40 drops of valerian root extract mixed with water was equal to one of my anti-anxiety pills. When I started to feel anxious, I'd take 25 drops of valerian root and I would feel calmer, more able to manage myself. This felt like a huge victory to me after all my time spent bombed out on pills that made me feel like a zombie.

The effect of my childhood experiences on me became clear and every awakened memory began to *feel like the removal of yet another layer of my pain. It took me ten long years to remove each layer and each time I did, it felt like I was saying goodbye to a loved one, someone comfortable and familiar. At times this made me sad, but not enough to give up my quest to be the person I truly was. My fears were my way of running away from the realities of life, forcing me to choose the easy way out. But I didn't want the easy way out anymore so when I finally faced a fear and released it, I was left with a question of "well now what?" I had to learn a new way of facing my life without my fear to hide behind.*

I also came to the realization that in releasing all of these unwanted elements from my life, I had a lot of empty space to fill within me. I chose new hobbies, new interests, and, most of all, a new mindset. In a way, I guess you could say that I did a lot of detoxification of my inner being. Through this process, I learned that when I lose sight of myself, I open the door to unwanted situations. But I have chosen to embrace myself and embrace my life.

Alexandra

The night after I received that letter, Jack and I sat together in the gazebo, sharing a bottle of wine. He listened quietly as I told him about the letter and about how I felt such a connection to this woman whom I'd never met. When I was done, he took my hand in his and we sat together, sipping our wine as I played her letters and phone calls over and over in my head.

"I don't mean to change the subject," Jack said after a while, "but you haven't heard from your friends in a while, have you?"

"No, everyone has been busy lately. I'll call Francesca tomorrow though, maybe she's free for lunch this weekend."

"You two had a really close relationship, didn't you?" Jack asked. "I mean, compared to Annie and Judy. I know you're all close, but you and Francesca seemed to have more of a connection than the others."

I nodded.

"We were inseparable in school, always so close, telling each other everything," I said.

"And now?" Jack asked.

"I'm so glad we've reconnected over these last several months but she seems more guarded now, more than she ever used to be," I said. "But I guess I'm not really the same person I once was either." I thought for a moment. "We clicked on the first day we met," I said. "We met when we were 13 and we loved each other immediately."

"That's really something," Jack said. "I wish I had a friend like that."

"What about me?' I asked with mock hurt in my voice and grin on my face.

"I mean a male friend, a buddy. You are so much more than just a friend, you're my best friend, my life, my lover, my world," he said, pulling me in to kiss him. Even now, after all this time, I could feel his kiss all the way down in my toes. Sitting in the gazebo with Jack, where we'd said "I do", surrounded by Francesca's flowers, I felt so happy and safe and engulfed in love.

I hadn't been able to get hold of Francesca to meet up that weekend and the following week was scheduled tightly with back to back patients. I knew the rest of the staff was similarly busy so I arrived on Monday morning with coffee and bagels for the whole office. The receptionist hurried over to give me a hand. As we took everything to the break room, she informed me that I had a patient waiting in my office.

"What?" I asked, a little annoyed. "I thought I didn't have any appointments for at least another thirty minutes."

"She doesn't have an appointment but she insisted she had to see you today, right now," the receptionist said apologetically.

"Does Jack know about this?" I asked.

"Yes, he's the one who okayed it," she said.

"This is completely unacceptable, you can't just leave people in my office when I'm not there," I snapped. "I could have patient files open on my desk, confidential files. You know the rules."

"I'm sorry," she stammered. I saw the look on her face and I suddenly felt terrible for how I'd spoken to her.

"No, I'm sorry," I said, more patiently this time. "I shouldn't have talked to you like that. But in the future, no one goes into my office without me--and I mean no one."

"Of course, Dr. I'm sorry," the receptionist apologized again. I gave her a friendly squeeze on the arm to show I wasn't mad anymore.

"So who is it?" I asked as I turned to leave.

"She wouldn't give me her last name, but she said her name was Alexandra."

I froze.

"Alexandra? Are you sure?" I asked. The receptionist nodded and I hurried out of the break room. I opened my office door and stared in amazement at the lithe woman standing by my window, silhouetted by the morning light. She turned to face me when I opened the door and I gasped.

"Francesca my darling girl." Pulling her into my arms.

Printed in the United States
By Bookmasters